Timothy
TALKS TO JESUS

IRENE J. STEELE

AS/IS Press
Huntsville, AL

Timothy Talks to Jesus
Published by AS/IS Press
P.O. Box 365
Madison, AL 35758
www.irenejsteele.com

Text and Illusrations copyright © 2021 by Irene J. Steele.

All Rights Reserved. This book or parts thereof may not be reproduced in any form, stored in a retrieval system, or transmitted in any form by any means—electronic, mechanical, photocopy, recording, or otherwise—without prior written permission of the publisher, except as provided by United States of America copyright law.

ISBN: 978-0-578-31933-9

Library of Congress Control Number: 2021922338

Interior design by Echelon House Publishing
Illustrations by Artist Jason Langford
Cover Design by hellonaomi

20 21 22 23 24 — 9 8 7 6 5 4 3 2 1

Printed in the United States of America

For Tony

You are God's special gift just for me. Your unselfish love and devotion is a treasure that I get to experience each day of my life. I love you.

Juanita Smith

Thank you, Mom, for encouraging me in my love of literature!

To All

"You will seek me and find me when you seek me with all your heart."
—Jeremiah 29:13 NIV

Thank You...

Mark, for being an awesome friend, editor, and the brother that I never had.
Judy, for allowing God to use you.
Jason Langford, for your beautiful illustrations.
Echelon House Publishing, for bringing this story to life.

"How can I talk to Jesus?" Timothy asked his mother.

"Hmmm?" Lynn diced onions and green peppers for Sunday's dinner.

"How can I talk to Jesus and He talk back to me?" Timothy patted her leg.

"Talk to Jesus?" She wiped the corner of her eye. "Give me a minute, sweetie." She ran to the sink to flush her eyes with water.

"I've got to get this onion out of my eye!" she wailed.

Timothy walked into the living room to his sister Alyssa.

"Lyssa, how can I talk to Jesus?"

Alyssa was coloring a ballerina. "Don't step on my crayons!"

Timothy carefully stepped over the crayons and sat down.

"I want to talk to Jesus," he said.

"Jesus?" Alyssa whispered. She put the crayons back into the box.

"Yes."

"Are you gonna tell Him I hit you?"

Timothy shook his head.

"Okay. Mommy said He's all around."

Timothy looked over his shoulder. "Where?" he whispered.

"I don't know. All around." Alyssa waved her hand in the air as she picked up another crayon and turned back to her drawing.

Timothy looked for his father. Alex's eyes were glued to the television.

"Daddy?"

"Yes, son?"

"I wanna talk to Jesus."

"Yes! Touchdown!"

Alex yelled at the television and swung his son in the air.

"Uh, okay. What do you want to talk to Him about?"

"I wanna tell Him something."

"Well, you can tell Him at night when you say your prayers."

"He only talks at night?"

"Uh no, of course not. Why don't you talk with Mommy about it?"

"Mommy's washing her eye."

"Look! Here come your cousins Amber and Mary!"
Alex got up to answer the door.

"Hey, old man!" He fist-bumped his brother-in-law, C. G.

"Coming in with a hot plate!" Nicole breezed into the room carrying a covered dish.

Timothy tugged on his aunt's skirt. "Auntie, can you help me talk to…"

"I'm going to put this down and come back for my kisses." Nicole winked at Timothy and hurried past him.

Alyssa led her cousins to her room. Timothy lagged behind.

"Where are we going?" Amber asked.

"To my room," Alyssa replied.

Alyssa motioned for Timothy to speak.

"I want to talk to Jesus," Timothy told Amber.

"Is that all? If you want to talk to Jesus, you have to talk like He talks."

"How does He talk?" Timothy whispered.

"Like they talk in church." Amber said a few strange words.

Alyssa and Timothy stared at her.

"That's how Jesus talks?" Timothy asked.

Amber nodded.

"You have to be swain first," Mary piped in. "In your spirit."

"What?" All three looked at Mary.

"Ha ha," Amber laughed. "She means 'slain.' Slain in the spirit. It's 'slain,' not swain." Amber laughed again.

"What's slain?" Alyssa asked.

"You have to fall out," Amber explained.

"Fall out?"

Amber dropped to the floor and closed her eyes.

Lynn opened the door. "What are you all doing in here? Amber, get up off of the floor."

"Nothing," they answered in unison.

Lynn opened the door wide. "Good. Come into the living room. We're going to eat pretty soon."

"This looks delicious." Alex took off his Alabama cap and bowed to his wife.

"Everybody," he reached out his hand and blessed the food.

"I want a drumstick." Alyssa pointed to the fried chicken.

"'May I please have a drumstick?'" Lynn corrected.

"May I…" Timothy began.

"Yes, son?" Alex asked.

"What do you want, baby?" Lynn smiled at her son.

All eyes focused on Timothy.

"Two pieces of orange pie!"

"Me, too!" Mary agreed.

"The sweet potato pies are for dessert," Lynn laughed with everyone.

After dinner, Amber sat cross-legged on Alyssa's bed. "Remember," she instructed. "You start with Scripture. Then you pray."

"Before He talks back?" Timothy asked.

"Yes."

"Amber! Mary! We're about to go," Nicole called.

After saying their goodbyes, Alex and Lynn turned to Alyssa and Timothy. "Okay, you two. Bath and bedtime. Precious, get ready for your bath with me and prayer with Daddy."

"And..." Alex turned to Timothy.

"My bath with you and pray with Mommy!"

"Mommy?" Alyssa raised her arm to be washed. "Tee Tee wants to talk to Jesus. Can you help him?"

"Yes, baby." Lynn kissed her daughter. "Daddy and I will help him."

"Look what I made!" Alyssa showed off her handful of bubbles.

"Okay, son. Who's gonna help fight the dirt battle tonight?"

Timothy pointed to a yellow and red sailboat.

Alex poured bubble bath into the flowing water. They watched the boat wobble over the foam.

"Son, sometimes when God speaks to us, we don't always hear Him."

"Why? Because we've been bad?"

"No. Many times, God speaks to our heart and not our ears." Alex touched Timothy's chest. "Sometimes God will let you feel His presence on the inside."

"Okay," said Timothy.

Lynn opened her arms to Timothy. "Did you have a good bath?"

"Yes. Me and Daddy sailed my boat. Daddy tried to attack my boat, but we got away."

"Sweetie, I know that you want to talk to Jesus, and that's a beautiful thing. God speaks to us in many different ways."

"But how can I tell?"

"You can tell in here." She touched his chest.

"That's what Daddy said."

Timothy knelt with his mother. "I want to pray first," he said.

"Okay."

"Close your eyes."

"Yes, sir." Lynn closed her eyes and bowed her head.

"Dear God..." Timothy whispered.

Lynn pulled the comforter over Timothy and kissed him goodnight.

"Love you, son."

"Love you, too," Timothy repeated.

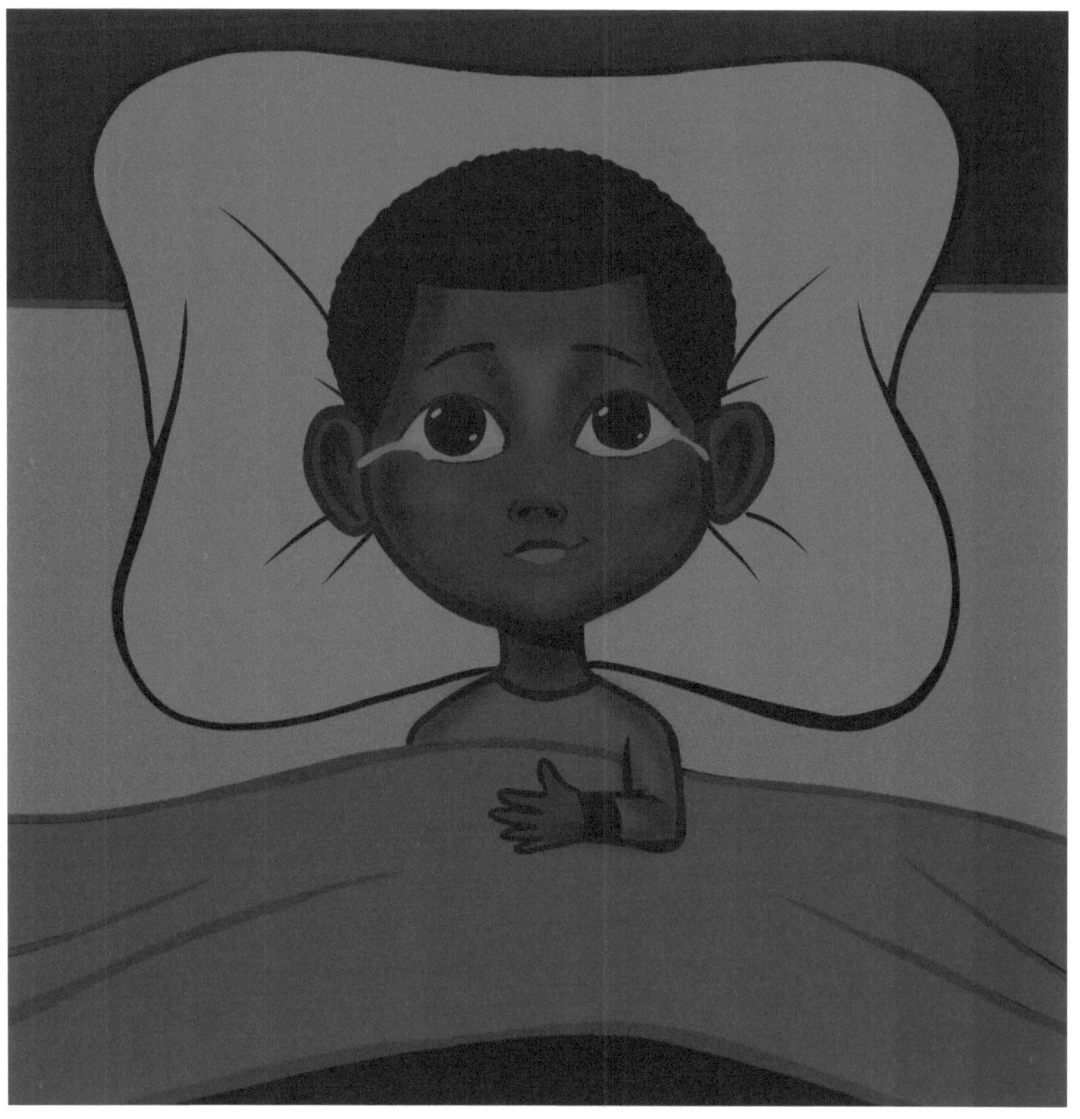

Timothy lay on his side and looked at the curtains covering his window. He turned on his back and stared at the ceiling.

"Jesus," he whispered. "Will you talk with me?"

"I need to tell you…" he started as the tears came. "…Something," he continued. He felt warm inside.

His heart felt like it was singing.

"I love you," he choked out.

It was enough.

He talked to Jesus… and Jesus talked back.